If You Are a Kaka,
You Eat Doo Doo

and other poop tales from nature

Sara Martel

illustrated by
Sara Lynn Cramb

Peachtree

Hey all you potty poopers, your flushing puzzles us.

See this mound?

Humans call it ca-ca, or doo-doo, or number two, or poo, or poop, or even dingleberries.

Whatever you call it, you flush it away as fast as you can.

Not us.

We use it.

Poops help us hairy-nosed wombats talk. Instead of voice messages, we leave messages with box-shaped poops.

Why?

Round poo rolls, but square *scat* stays put, telling other wombats where we live.

The wombat's trail is marked with poops.

The wombat may be a cuddly-looking *herbivore*, but it's as heavy as a pit bull, and a riled-up wombat with a running start can knock down a grown-up human!

When threatened by a *predator*, the wombat scrambles headfirst down its burrow, plugging the passage with its *cartilage*-reinforced hind end and sometimes kicking with its muscular back legs.

We baby golden tortoise beetles pile our poo on our backs and crawl around wearing it.

Why?

A coating of poop helps us beetle *larvae* hide from animals that might eat us.

Adult golden tortoise beetles are the size of your pinky nail and can make quick color changes from gleaming gold to orange or brown.

Look for them on the plants they eat—morning glories, bindweeds, and sweet potato leaves.

The baby beetle uses its anal tube to squeeze poop onto its back, forming a fecal shield.

If the disguise fails, the larva can flip up its shield to block an attack.

The chicks of many bird species make *fecal sacs* like this one. Some parents even eat the sacs!

We baby black-capped chickadees poop out our poos in a clear, gooey package called a *fecal sac* that our parents carry away.

Why?

Because that makes it harder for hungry raccoons or squirrels to find our homes with their noses.

Chickadees pack information about lurking dangers into their calls. One call says that an owl is nearby, and a change in the song might mean that a ground predator such as a cat is approaching.

We silver-spotted skipper caterpillars can shoot our poops 38 times our body length. If we were as big as you, we'd be able to shoot our poops past four school buses lined up in a long row!

Why do we sling our poo?

So any caterpillar eater finding our droppings is a long way from finding us.

A caterpillar-eating assassin bug closes in.

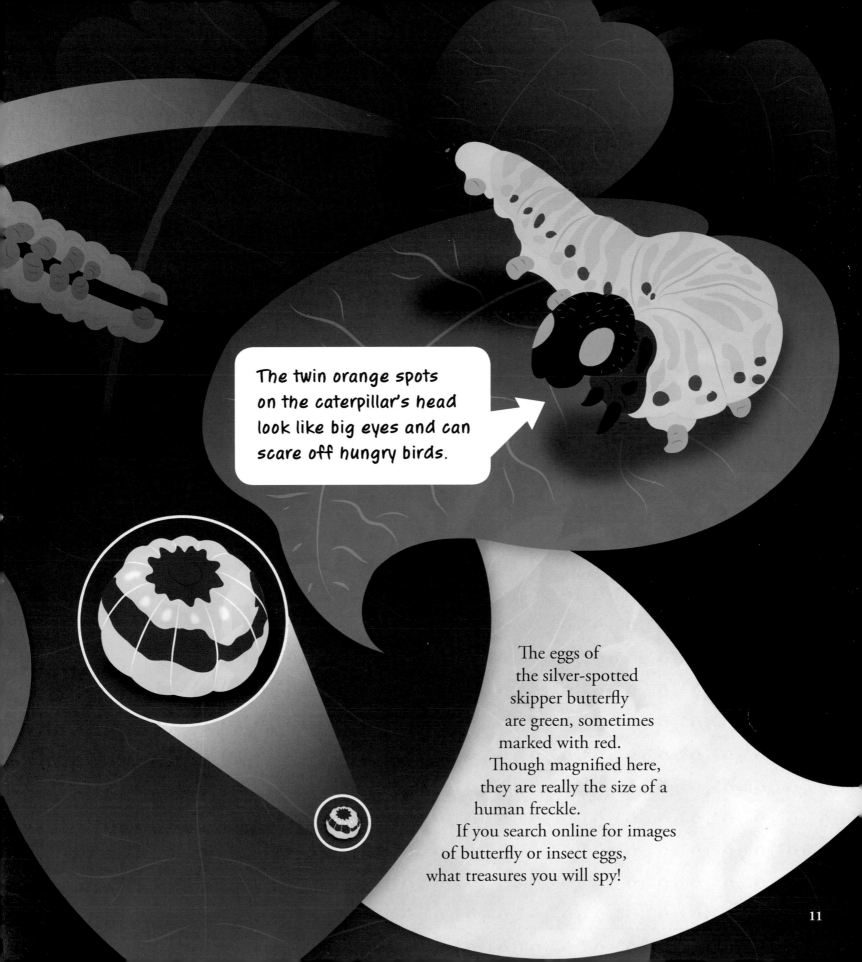

The twin orange spots on the caterpillar's head look like big eyes and can scare off hungry birds.

The eggs of the silver-spotted skipper butterfly are green, sometimes marked with red. Though magnified here, they are really the size of a human freckle. If you search online for images of butterfly or insect eggs, what treasures you will spy!

We baby hoopoes shoot poo, too. Our back ends are like squirt guns, pooping right into the eyes of whoever bothers us.

Why?

Because a well-aimed poop missile can chase off a predator. After all, who wants *feces* in their faces?

Besides spurting poop, baby hoopoes and their moms have another stinky defense.

Inside their *preen glands* they brew a brown stew that smells like rotting meat, and when they spread the disgusting oily stuff through their feathers, few predators want to eat them.

13

We shoebills squirt our poo all over our legs—on purpose!

Why?

We can't sweat, so pooping on our legs cools us when strong sunlight strikes.

Some storks, vultures, and seabirds also sometimes relieve themselves upon their legs and feet.

The shoebill's huge bill helps it bulldoze face first through marshy water to seize large prey, such as a lungfish that's as long as your leg.

We gidgee skink lizards all march to the same spot in our rocky neighborhood to *defecate*.

Why?

By piling our scat together, we send a powerful message to passing skinks that we are the gidgee skink tribe that lives here!

If you had this skink's sniffing skills, you could tell your best buddy's poop from any stranger's droppings by smelling it! Gidgee skinks live in communities of up to sixteen members, often relatives.

A skink sniffs with help from its tongue.

A close-up view of a scale insect attached to bark, with a honeydew drop at the end of its long anal tube.

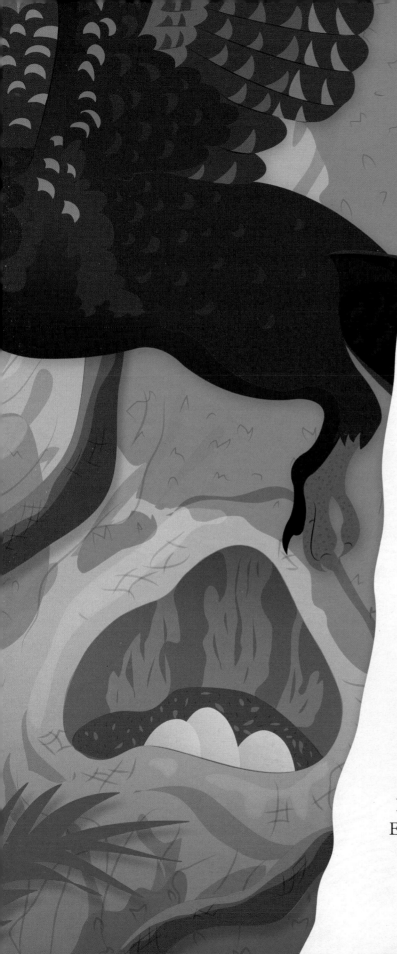

If you are a kaka, you eat doo-doo!

Why?

Because it's delicious! This sweet poo from **scale insects** is called **honeydew**. It helps us female kakas build energy to lay our eggs.

Kakas press their bristly tongues into the hearts of flowers to blot up **pollen** and **nectar**. Since some pollen sticks to their bills and gets carried to other flowers, these parrots serve as forest **pollinators**.

Kaka populations are declining, and their rivalry with a European wasp for honeydew may be one reason why.

We baby Ozark blind cave salamanders eat gray bat doo-doo.

Why?!

Because there's not much else to eat in a cave. The gray bats do us a favor by pooping snacks in our home.

Ozark blind cave salamanders can see as larvae, but as they transform into adults and wriggle deeper into the dark caves, their eyelids seal shut. Adults use smell to find prey and can sense nearby movements through special lines of sensory cells along the sides of their bodies.

If you are a male MacGregor's bowerbird, you collect caterpillar droppings and decorate your **bower** with them.

Why?

Making art with caterpillar poops and other treasures helps us male MacGregor's bowerbirds impress female bowerbirds.

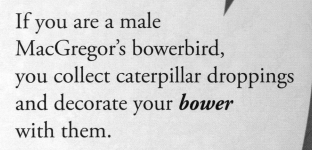

Not every male bowerbird collects insect doo-doo, also called *frass*. Many gather flowers, while some favor bits of fruit they puke up, small skulls, or even pieces of *mammal* scat for display.

The satin bowerbird shown here is one of 20 species of bowerbirds.
His favorite color?
One guess!

Caterpillar poo dangles like ornaments in his bower as a MacGregor's bowerbird (left) dances for a lady.

We common waxbills collect **_carnivore_** poo—especially the **_scat_** of servals—and tuck it inside and around our nests.

Why?

The scary stench of carnivore scat helps keep other animals from snacking on our eggs.

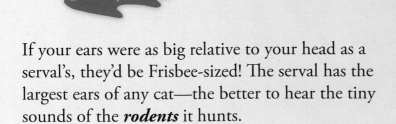

If your ears were as big relative to your head as a serval's, they'd be Frisbee-sized! The serval has the largest ears of any cat—the better to hear the tiny sounds of the **_rodents_** it hunts.

To poop, the sloth clambers down from its treetop and digs a potty hole in the ground with its stubby tail.

We brown-throated three-toed sloths only defecate about once a week.

Why?

We need a jumbo stomach and a long time to digest all the leaves we eat, and pooping less often helps us keep turning plants into fuel to live.

The moths in a sloth's fur may provide nutrients for the algae growing there.

Mossy-green *algae* thrive in the fur of a brown-throated three-toed sloth, helping it blend with leaves and stay hidden. Moths also live in the fur and lay their eggs in the sloth's poop.

We doodlebugs don't poop until we grow up, and sometimes that takes one to three years.

What a doozie of a doo-doo we doodlebugs first do!

Why?

Our hind ends are busy making silk—mostly for our *cocoons*—so poop is blocked from reaching our *anuses*.

We doodlebugs must hold all doo-doo until we change into winged adults.

Antlion *meconiums* can appear pinkish, shiny, and jellybean-like.

Hiding droppings inside their bodies may help some insects keep their dwellings more secret.

The antlion's poo pellet is called a *meconium*, which is also the name of the first doo-doo that you pooped as a newborn human.

This captured ant slides toward the waiting doodlebug.

Buried in sand beneath the trap it dug, a doodlebug (also called an antlion *larva*) ambushes prey.

Okay, all you potty flushers, are you wondering what human poop could be used for?

A decoration to dangle in your living room? **That's a terrible idea!**

A dandy disguise? **That idea is even worse!**

A territory marker for proud display on your lawn? **No, no, no!**

Wait, what's that you say?
Engineers are making jet fuel from poop?

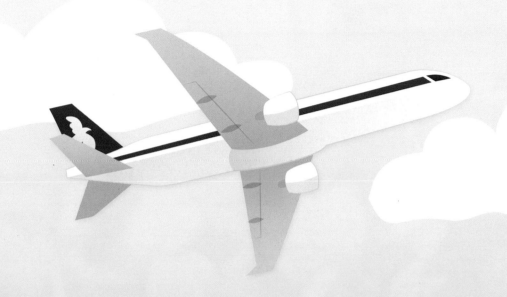

Wowza!! Potty poopers propelled sky-high in poo-powered planes!

Now you are talking!

YAHOO, DOO-DOO!!!

Cast of Characters

Pages 4 – 5:

Southern hairy-nosed wombat ●
Lasiorhinus latifrons

Range: parts of Australia

Also pictured:

Dingo ●
Canis lupus dingo

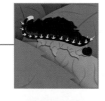

Pages 6 – 7:

Golden tortoise beetle ●
Charidotella sexpunctata
(previously called *Metriona bicolor*)

Range: large parts of North America and
parts of Central and South America

Also pictured:

Black carpenter ant ●
Camponotus pennsylvanicus

Pages 8 – 9:

Black-capped chickadee ●
Poecile atricapillus

Range: large parts of the northern U.S.
and southern Canada

Also pictured:

Eastern screech-owl ●
Megascops asio

Domestic cat ●
Felis catus

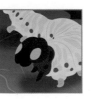

Pages 10 – 11:

Silver-spotted skipper ●
Epargyreus clarus
Range: much of the U.S. and parts of
southern Canada and northern Mexico

Also pictured:

Wheel bug (a species of assassin bug) ●
Arilus cristatus

Pages 12 – 13:

Hoopoe ●
Upupa epops

Range: large parts of Africa, Asia,
and Europe

Also pictured:

Red fox ●
Vulpes vulpes

Pages 14 – 15:

Shoebill ●
Balaeniceps rex

Range: parts of central Africa

Also pictured:

African lungfish, ●
also called marbled lungfish
Protopterus aethiopicus

White-faced whistling duck ●
Dendrocygna viduata

Sitatunga, also called marshbuck ●
Tragelaphus spekii

Common waxbill ●
Estrilda astrild

Pages 16 – 17:

Gidgee skink ●
Egernia stokesii

Range: parts of Australia

Pages 18 – 19:

Kaka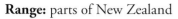
Nestor meridionalis meridionalis
(the South Island subspecies)

Range: parts of New Zealand

Also pictured:

Sooty beech scale insect ●
Ultracoelostoma assimile

Pages 20 –21:

Ozark blind cave salamander ●
Eurycea spelaea

Range: the Ozark region of the U.S.,
which includes parts of Missouri, Arkansas,
Oklahoma, and Kansas

Also pictured:

Gray bat ●
Myotis grisescens

A species of rove beetle ●
Sepidophilus littorinus

Common pill bug ●
(a species of isopod), also called roly-poly
Armadillidium vulgare

Shagreen snail ●
Inflectarius inflectus

Pages 22 – 23:

MacGregor's bowerbird ●
Amblyornis macgregoriae

Range: parts of the island of New Guinea

Also pictured:

Satin bowerbird ●
Ptilonorhynchus violaceus

Pages 24 – 25:

Common waxbill ●
Estrilda astrild

Range: large parts of Africa south of the
Sahara desert; has also been introduced to
Spain, Hawaii, and elsewhere

Also pictured:

Serval ●
Leptailurus serval

African pygmy mouse ●
Mus minutoides

African house snake ●
Lamprophis fuliginosus

Pages 26 – 27:

Brown-throated three-toed sloth ●
Bradypus variegatus

Range: parts of Central and South America

Also pictured:

A species of sloth moth ●
Cryptoses choloepi

Pages 28 – 29:

Antlion ●
(A North American species in the genus
Myrmeleon is pictured.)

Range: the common antlion
(*Myrmeleon immaculatus*)
lives in the eastern and southern U.S.;
over 2,000 species of antlion live worldwide

Also pictured:

Trap-jaw ant ●
Odontomachus brunneus

Meconium from a threadwing antlion ●
(*Dielocroce hebraea*)

Glossary

algae (singular = alga): A plant-like life form that often lives in water.

anal tube: The hind portion of some insects' bodies. At its tail end sits the anal opening, or anus, through which the insect poops.

anus: The poop exit in humans and many other animals.

bacteria (singular = bacterium): A single-celled life form too tiny to see with the naked eye. Many bacteria help animals (including people) in various ways, while others can make them ill.

bower: A structure built of sticks and other objects by a male bowerbird, where he shows off his treasures and skills.

carnivore: An animal that eats mostly other animals, either by killing them or finding them dead. A consumer of dead animals is called a *scavenger*.

cartilage: Tough animal tissue, harder than flesh but more flexible than bones.

cloaca: The poop exit in many animals, including birds and reptiles, which is the same hole that eggs exit from.

cocoon: A cover made by some insect larvae from silk to guard them while changing into adult form.

defecate: To poop.

fecal sac: A gooey covering produced by certain young birds to contain their poops.

fecal shield: A cover made at least partly of poop by larvae of certain beetle species, held on top or behind the body.

feces: Poop.

frass: Another name for insect poop, or *droppings*.

guano: Another name for bat *scat* or seabird poop.

herbivore: An animal that eats plants.

honeydew: Waste created by certain insects after feeding on sap. Sugary and watery, it feeds other wildlife, including some species of ants, hummingbirds, and woodpeckers.

larvae (singular = larva): The young forms of many animals, including butterflies, salamanders, and beetles. Larvae *transform*, or go through big changes, to become adults—a process also known as *metamorphosis*.

mammal: An animal whose young feed on milk made by their mother's body. Wombats and humans are examples of mammals.

meconium: The first poop left by certain insect larvae upon transforming into adults. Also the name of a human infant's first poop after being born.

nectar: A sweet drink made by flowers to invite pollinators.

pollen: A powder made by plants to help them make more plants.

pollinator: An animal that helps plants make more plants by moving pollen.

predator: An animal that kills and eats other animals.

preen gland: Many birds have this small body part, which sits just above the tail and produces a waxy oil. The bird dabs this spot during preening in order to spread the oil through its feathers, like conditioner.

protein: A kind of nutrient necessary for animal growth; meat, eggs, and nuts contain lots of protein.

rodents: Mice, rats, squirrels, and their close relatives.

scale insects: A widespread family of small insects including 8,000 known species.

scat: Animal poop.

Poo-Powered Planes and Other Doo-Doo Doings

Future airline flights might be powered partly by **biofuel** made from plant material and animal poop—and that's just one of the many uses that people are inventing for poop.

At Fair Oaks Farms in Indiana, the **dung** (animal poo) of 35,000 cows is vacuumed up and moved into **biodigesters**. Inside the chambers, as in stomachs, bacteria break down doo-doo into methane gas (one of the non-smelly gases in your farts) and fertilizer. The gas powers a fleet of forty tanker trucks to haul the farm's milk, and the fertilizer nourishes crops that feed the cows.

Using poop as fuel is not a new idea. Livestock dung (also called **manure**, or **cow patties**, or **meadow muffins**) has for centuries been burned around the world for cooking and heating.

Like the MacGregor's bowerbird, some humans even use dung for decoration. In Maine and elsewhere, moose doo-doo is collected and coated with glossy preservative, then made into necklaces and earrings to sell to tourists. The Miller Park Zoological Society in Bloomington, Illinois has raised more than $50,000 by collecting poop from its reindeer and selling it as handmade glitter-coated Christmas ornaments called Magical Reindeer Gems.

People are putting human poop to good use, too. Some of it, after being processed in a waste treatment facility, is used to fertilize athletic fields, parks, and golf courses. In Africa, inventive Kenyan teen Leroy Mwasaru and four of his buddies set out to conquer several of their school's challenges at once. Overcoming grownups' doubts, they put a biodigester to work converting the students' poop, which was polluting nearby drinking water, into gas (mostly methane) for cooking fuel. This has saved trees that school workers were cutting down to burn. The kids call their biodigestor a **human-waste bioreactor**.

And in Haiti, two women hope to solve a poop problem using composting toilets. Through their nonprofit organization SOIL (Sustainable Organic Integrated Livelihoods), scientist Sasha Kramer and her engineer friend Sarah Brownell dream of making these toilets available to the two and a half billion people worldwide who lack access to clean pooping options. Water is saved because the toilets need no flushing, and human poop that otherwise pollutes the land and water is collected and composted with plant scraps to make rich soil for growing crops.

Where other people see problems, Leroy, Sasha, Sarah, and others see possibilities—resources to create cooking fuel and nutrients to revive poor soils. What possibilities might you imagine on your next flush? Whatever they might be, I hope you find the everlasting delight in nature that I have. I hope we are all inspired to honor and tend our planet. And I hope that Earth may forever be graced with wondrous creatures—kakas included.

Acknowledgments

The author thanks the following people for their help during her research: Mark Swanson, Professor Michael Bull of Flinders University, Betsy Williams, Professor John Oswald of Texas A&M University, Richard Greene of the Smithsonian Institution Natural History Library, Charley Eiseman (author of Tracks & Signs of Insects and Other Invertebrates), Dr. Clifford B. Frith, and Dr. Dawn W. Frith.

Tilbury House Publishers
12 Starr Street
Thomaston, Maine 04861
800-582-1899 • www.tilburyhouse.com

Hardcover ISBN 978-088448-488-2
eBook ISBN 978-9-88448-498-1

15 16 17 18 19 20 XXX 10 9 8 7 6 5 4 3 2 1

Library of Congress Cataloging-in-Publication Data

Names: Martel, Sara, 1965- author. | Cramb, Sara Lynn, illustrator.
Title: If you are a Kaka, you eat doo-doo : and other poop tales from nature

/ by Sara Martel ; illustrated by Sara Lynn Cramb.
Description: Thomaston, Maine : Tilbury House Publishers, [2016] | Audience:

Ages 6-11.
Identifiers: LCCN 2016000035 | ISBN 9780884484882 (hardcover)
Subjects: LCSH: Animal droppings--Juvenile literature. | Animal
  behavior--Juvenile literature.
Classification: LCC QL768 .M3735 2016 | DDC 591.5--dc23 LC record available
at http://lccn.loc.gov/2016000035

Designed by Sara Lynn Cramb and Kathy Squires

January 2016 / Plant & Location Shenzhen Caimei Printing Co., Shenzhen, China
Job/Batch #55962-0 / SCP 121915.5

Dedications

To my siblings, Susanna Morrill and Dave and Matt Lenoe,
and to all the nonhuman animals I've ever cared for—
you soulful beings—my heart is yours forever.— *Sara Martel*

To my husband, Justin, for his limitless support
and encouragement,
and to all of the amazing and inspiring creatures
that live on this planet.— *Sara Lynn Cramb*

Sara Martel

Sara Martel endured many close encounters with poop
during her eleven years as a zookeeper at the St. Louis Zoo—
always from animals that were dear to her,
including the multiple fly-by poop droppings
she received from rainbow lorikeets.
She served, too, as an assistant field biologist helping with seabird
research for organizations including the U.S. Fish & Wildlife Service.
Sara has since written about wildlife conservation efforts for regional
and national publications including *Sierra*, *National Wildlife*, *Birder's
World*, *Birding*, and the *Boston Globe Magazine*.
Her husband Rick, along with Scout the dog and Maverick the cat,
were treated to countless dinnertime poop tales during this book's writing.

Sara Lynn Cramb

Sara Lynn Cramb grew up in the Great Lakes region,
where she spent much of her time adventuring in the woods,
drawing, playing with four-legged friends, and reading picture books.
She has created illustrations and designs for numerous
educational books, interactive signage, posters, and children's books.
Sara shares her home with her husband, two grumpy turtles, a pair of
mischievous cats, and far more books than one person should own.
Her children's book illustrations include
50 Things You Should Know About the Human Body
and *Smithsonian Young Explorers Fact Book and Floor Puzzle: 50 States*.